D1611742

NEW POEMS: 1980-88

NEW POEMS: 1980-88

by John Haines

STORY LINE PRESS

1990

Publication of this work is made possible in part by grants from the National Endowment for the Arts, and the generous support of the Nicholas Roerich Museum and the Western States Art Federation

The Western States Book Awards are a project of the Western States Arts Federation. The Awards are sponsored by "Corporate Founder" The Xerox Foundation, the Lannan Foundation, Crane Duplicating Service, and the Witter Bynner Foundation for Poetry. Additional funding is provided by the National Endowment for the Arts Literature program.

811
H15n

PS
3558
.A33
N49
1990

ISBN: 0-934257-44-2   Cloth   0-934257-45-0   Paper

AL

Book design and front cover painting by Lysa McDowell

Published by Story Press, Inc.
d.b.a. Story Line Press
Three Oaks Farm
Brownsville, Oregon
97327-9718

The author wishes to thank the following organizations for financial support during the period in which many of these poems were written:

The John Simon Guggenheim Memorial Foundation (1984-85)
Alaska State Council on the Arts (1987-88)
The Ingram Merrill Foundation (1987-88)

Special thanks to Crane Duplicating Service, Inc. for providing our galleys

ACKNOWLEDGEMENTS

The poems in this book originally appeared in these
publications whose editors I would like to thank.

ZYZZYVA   "Meditation On A Skull Carved In Crystal"

ARK, NER/BLQ, PUSHCART ANNUAL   "Rain Country"

THE HUDSON REVIEW   "Death And The Miser"
                      (parts II, III, IV, V)
NER/BLQ   (parts I, VI)
PERMAFROST   (early versions of parts of the poem)

OHIO REVIEW   "Days of Edward Hopper"

THE HUDSON REVIEW   "Head Of Sorrow, Head Of Thought"

IRONWOOD   "Of Michelangelo, His Question"

POETRY EAST   "On A Certain Field In Auvers"

NER/BLQ, ALASKA QUARTERLY   "Paolo And Francesca"

NEW VIRGINIA REVIEW   "Broken Mirrors"

ALASKA QUARTERLY   "The Owl In The Mask Of The Dreamer"
NER/BLQ ANTHOLOGY
(poem originally titled "From The Workshop Of Brancusi And Giacometti"),

NER/BLQ ANTHOLOGY, SLACKWATER REVIEW
                      "Ancestor Of The Hunting Heart"

ORCA   "Little Cosmic Dust Poem"

CLOCKWATCH REVIEW   Water Of Night"   and
                      "Forest Without Leaves"
HIGH COUNTRY NEWS
KANSAS QUARTERLY
AMICUS JOURNAL
RACCOON
ORCA

CONTENTS

Introduction   i

Little Cosmic Dust Poem   1

I
Meditation On a Skull Carved In Crystal

I	"To think that the world"	5
II	"Within the artifact"	6
III	"Where there is nothing"	7
IV	"No one the color of darkness"	8
V	"Blood into ice, and fur"	9
VI	"Burn sacrifice, for all"	10
VII	"As if the pain of thought"	12
VIII	"Of the dissolution"	13
IX	"Intelligence is what we find"	14

II
Tenderfoot   17

Rain Country

I	"The woods are sodden"	18
II	"Light in the aspen wood"	20
III	"Shadows blur in the rain"	21
IV	"And all the stammering folly"	23
V	"Much rain has fallen"	24
VI	"I write this down"	25

III

Death and The Miser
I	"God surely sees us"	29
II	"The dream within the acorn"	31
III	"You would never willingly wear"	32
IV	"Believe in the angel beside you"	34
V	"So much leaden weight"	35
VI	"Be comforted, for your companions"	36

IV

Days of Edward Hopper
I	"These are the houses that stand"	41
II	"Tell me, you who were close"	42
III	"Obedience to Sundays drilled us"	44
IV	"Sleepwalker, your footsteps"	45
V	"A trolley bell clangs"	46
VI	"And once for me also"	47

V

Head Of Sorrow, Head Of Thought	51

| **Of Michelangelo, His Question** | 52 |

On A Certain Field In Auvers
I	"On the road to hallucination"	54
II	"I, who never for one hour"	56
III	"In the asylum of Saint Rémy"	57

| **Paolo And Francesca** | 58 |

Broken Mirrors
I	"If what you say of the majestic"	59
II	"Into your blue forgetfulness"	60
III	"I...I... am the woman"	61
IV	"But when all these shattered"	62

The Owl In The Mask Of The Dreamer 63

Ancestor Of The Hunting Heart 64

VI

Water Of Night

I	"Before any match was struck"	69
II	"The night people called to the shadows"	70
III	"From a few rocks ground into powder"	71
IV	"When the people of shadow"	72
V	"After the burden of soil"	73
VI	"We who found work for the dead"	74
VII	"Fire that was sunlight"	75
VIII	"Each of us brings a shadow"	76

VII

In The Forest Without Leaves

I	"In the forest without leaves..."	79
II	"What sounds can be heard"	80
III	"This earth written over with words"	81
IV	"One rock on another"	82
V	"Earth speech"	83
VI	"And sometimes through the air"	84
VII	"Say after me"	85
VIII	"Building with matches"	86
IX	"Those who write sorrow"	87
X	"Life was not a clock"	88
XI	"How the sun came to the forest"	89
XII	"In all the forest, chilled"	90
XIII	"What will be said of you"	91
XIV	"A coolness will come to their children"	92
XV	"In the forest without leaves"	93

John Haines is a man of character in the most American sense—solitary; strong. He has spent much of his life in wild country, and he has written of the wilderness with profound wonder, perception, and thanksgiving. He has given us an indispensable sense of our country, our continent, and our earth in his poems. His work, his whole work, enriches us.

1990 Western States Book Awards Jury Citation

Judges: Jorie Graham
Elizabeth Hardwick
William Kittredge
N. Scott Momaday

INTRODUCTION

BY DANA GIOIA

WHEN ROBINSON JEFFERS first saw the coast and mountains around Carmel in the fall of 1914, the discovery utterly transformed both him and his poetry. "For the first time in my life," Jeffers wrote years later, "I could see people living—amid magnificently unspoiled scenery—essentially as they did in the Idyls or the Sagas, or in Homer's Ithaca. Here was life purged of its ephemeral accretions. Men were riding after cattle, or plowing the headland, hovered by white sea-gulls, as they had done for thousands of years, and will for thousands of years to come. Here was contemporary life that was also permanent life." Other artists had enjoyed the grandeur of this particular landscape before Jeffers, but his identification went deeper than mere appreciation. He let what D.H. Lawrence called "the spirit of place" enter his imagination. Giving himself over to "this coast crying out for tragedy like all beautiful places," Jeffers was spiritually reborn. Isolated from literary life, spending part of the day in quiet manual labor, he mysteriously grew from an awkward literary apprentice into the West Coast's first great poet. Rooted in one specific landscape as deeply as any poet in American literature, Jeffers managed to create work which was both distinctly regional and unequivocally universal.

John Haines' decision in May of 1947 to move to Alaska had a similarly decisive effect on his life and work. Like many other young men who had come early to maturity during World War II, Haines had already had wide experience in life for someone still in his early twenties. The son of a naval officer, he had grown up "more or less homeless," moving from one military base to another. He had served in the wartime U.S. Navy and afterward had attended art school. But he had never known a sense of permanence in one specific place. Unexpectedly he found a center for his life on an isolated homestead in central Alaska.

He built a cabin on a deserted hillside above the Tanana River about seventy miles southeast of Fairbanks in a spot so remote that he claimed he could walk north from his homestead "all the way to the Arctic Ocean and never cross a road or encounter a village." Living alone much of the time, Haines spent twenty-five of the next forty-two years in the Alaskan interior. In the isolated countryside he had to become self-reliant largely supporting himself through hunting and trapping. "I began for the first time," he wrote thirty years later, "to make things for myself, to build shelters, to weave nets, to make sleds and harness, and to train animals for work. I learned to hunt, to watch, and to listen." A modern man resettled in the primal north, he had to relearn what his ancient ancestors knew—how to live off the land.

Haines also used the solitary years to master another primitive craft—making poems. Like Jeffers he came late to artistic maturity, and his development as a writer was inseparable from his creation of a life independent of the social and economic distractions of the modern city. Both men discovered their poetic identities in solitude, meditation, and hard physical labor. Haines' isolation, however, gave him personal authenticity only at the investment of many years. He was forty-two when his first book of poems, *Winter News*, was published by Wesleyan University Press in 1966. (His prose appeared even later; Haines was fifty-seven when his first book of essays, *Living Off the Country*, came out from University of Michigan Press in 1981.) Many young men, hoping to become writers, embark on romantic lives in the wilderness. But exhausted by responsibilities, unsupported by colleagues, and hungry for human society, few have the discipline to achieve their literary ambitions. Through patience, strength, and uncommon intelligence, Haines did. He is virtually unique among the significant poets of his generation in having emerged outside of either the university or an urban bohemia.

The growth of any artist's mind is ultimately private. But in Haines' case the years of silence and isolation make his development especially mysterious. While one might read his early poetry as a subjective record of the time, the most accessible account comes from his two books of essays, *Living Off the Country* (1981) and *The Stars, the Snow, the Fire* (1989).These superbly-written collections of mostly autobiographical prose reveal the importance of the dream-like solitude the empty Northern wilderness provided the author. By stepping out of the man-made rhythms of the city into the slower cycles of nature, Haines entered—perhaps unknowingly at first—a world of meditation. There are few overtly religious themes in Haines' writing, but both his poetry and prose are suffused with a sense of the sacred. What he sought in Alaska was the secular equivalent of what the early Christian hermits found in the Egyptian desert—the chance to build an authentic life *sub specie aeternitatis*. The synchronization with nature, the distance from the City of Man, the daily contemplation of solitary labor were all part of the spiritual discipline of the Desert Fathers. Haines may have lost the Catholicism of his childhood, but its vision of spiritual self-realization remained a guiding force in his adult life.

Normally I would not dwell on the circumstances of a living poet's background. The lives of most contemporary poets are too ordinary to shed much light on their work. But in Haines' case the connection between artist and art seems not only illuminating but inevitable. Reading his prose and poetry together, one feels the complete integrity of the author's life and work (and I use "integrity" here emphasizing its Latin root, *integer*, which means "wholeness"). Haines' poetry is rooted in the singular existence he chose. Essentially the same intelligence and sensibility consciously created both his adult life and his work. But to say that his verse is the natural expression of his values should not imply that it lacks artistry. The special splendor of Haines' poetry is that it honors experience without cheating literature. He mastered the craft of poetry without forgetting that art both originates in and returns to life.

The close connection between Haines' life and work, however, has led some critics to conflate the two. Focusing on the Alaskan elements in his work, they have sometimes reduced him to a regional writer. This view misunderstands the relationship between his prose and verse. As an essayist, Haines is a determined regionalist—a writer, that is, who stubbornly looks at the world from a fixed position. This sense of location gives Haines' prose real strength. It brings specificity to his judgments and roots his ideas in experience. But while Haines' earliest poetry focused almost entirely on Alaskan subject matter, his later books ranged far beyond local themes. He developed into a poet of broader interests who wrote as convincingly about Albert Pinkham Ryder or Arlington Cemetery as he did about glaciers and wolf packs.

If Haines is a regional poet, it is only in a secondary sense. For him outward subject matter is always less important than the inner moral vision it provokes. To reduce his poetry to regional affirmation, therefore, reveals nothing essential about its strengths. Likewise to represent him as an auto-biographical poet also misses his central preoccupations which are not so much personal as tribal. He is an obstinately visionary poet who characteristically transforms individual experience into universal human terms. One would be tempted to call him a philosophic poet if his imagination were not so frequently mythic. He deals in serious ideas, but the concepts are not presented abstractly. They are revealed in bare narrative terms like ancient legends, half obscured by time. Consider, for example, his short poem, "The Flight":

> It may happen again—this much
> I can always believe
> when our dawn fills with frightened neighbors
> and the ancient car refuses to start.
>
> The gunfire of locks and shutters
> echoes next door to the house
> left open
> for the troops that are certain to come.
>
> We shall leave behind nothing but cemeteries,
>
> and our life like a refugee cart
> overturned in the road,
> a wheel slowly spinning...

There is nothing overtly regional or autobiographical about this brief, apocalyptic poem. While it precisely describes the details of a particular scene, it leaves the actual location so vague it seems imaginary. The landscape is not rural but archetypically suburban. The experience presented is not personal but communal. The imminent danger is not from Nature but man. Likewise the poem dramatizes a specific incident without providing a broader narrative context. The private mythology in the background remains arcane. "The Flight" presents a nightmarish vision of a mysterious political disaster. Such quasi-mythic poems are at least as typical of Haines' *oeuvre* as his better-known Alaskan poems.

If Haines has chosen the North as the region of his poetry, it is not only a specific geographical area, but also the spiritual wilderness where the solitary imagination must confront existence without the comforting illusions of society. His North is a prophetic mountaintop from which the poet looks down on the corruption of the city. In this sense Haines is fundamentally a moral and political poet. If he has succeeded in his stated ambition of creating a poetry "so distinctive that it belongs to a certain place yet speaks for all places," it is because he speaks about matters important enough to transcend regional boundaries. His regionalism is not so much a fixed perspective as a point of departure for regions beyond. While his work may have originated in Alaska—biographically and thematically—it has never been confined by its birthplace.

Writing poetry in the Alaskan wilderness is a kind of pioneering as difficult as any other act of settlement. Finding an authentic way to articulate experiences new to literature is a formidable task. A young poet needs an imaginative foundation. Since there was little precedent in mainstream American poetry of the Forties and Fifties for the work Haines hoped to do, he had to discover his own set of models. Like most young poets of his generation, Haines was initially influenced by Pound, Eliot, and Williams, but gradually his search for masters went outside American literature. The confraternity of writers he eventually summoned to his remote Alaskan homestead was an unusual one. It included Tu Fu (as translated by Kenneth Rexroth), Li Po (from Pound's *Cathay*), Antonio Machado, Georg Trakl, and Robinson Jeffers. He also found inspiration in Scandinavian novelists like Knut Hamsun and Sigrid Undset whose fiction helped explain the North he had chosen as home.

An interesting study could be made of what Haines learned from each writer, but two important points need to be made. First, one must note how little his private canon resembled the common influences of his generation (though it did overlap with the models of two contemporaries the early Haines most resembled—Robert Bly and James Wright). Like Haines' lifestyle, his list of influences was unorthodox. The other significant point to be made about Haines' masters is how little of their direct influence one sees in his work. He did not begin publishing until he had assimilated their examples into a personal style. One can sense their presence only in subtle ways.

What one notices instead is the author's distinctive approach. His style is concise, intimate, but also very concentrated. If his syntax and diction are usually clear and simple, the way Haines organizes his images and ideas is complex.

The poems often move by leaps. Key pieces of information are left out, requiring the reader to fill in gaps of meaning. Perhaps the provocative combination of superficial clarity and deeper mystery is the greatest debt Haines owes to his European masters like Trakl and Machado.

Turning to Haines' *New Poems: 1980-88* after studying his earlier work, one sees both the continuity and innovation they provide. The recent work grows out of the style and concerns of his previous poetry. The language is still luminously clear, but the approach is no longer simple. The new poems are more complex and allusive. Whereas Haines' earlier work consisted mainly of short poems, his new book is built around six major sequences. These capacious new poems, however, remain rooted in the key elements of his earlier style. They use the compressed lyric of Haines' previous books as the building blocks of the ambitious sequences. Reading the new poems, one appreciates the masterful way the author uses concentrated lyric episodes to create expansive larger forms.

Significantly, there is little sense of regionalism in Haines' *New Poems*. Only one sequence refers directly to Alaska. If one views Haines' poetic development as a journey from the specific geography of the Alaskan wilderness to the uncharted places of the spirit, then that journey is now complete. The author no longer defines himself in relation to a particular location. When the wilderness appears in the new poems, it is as universal as Dante's dark wood. But if Haines now rejects his old identity as woodsman and hunter, he also displays more of his private artistic side—revealing something of the young man who forty years ago studied painting and sculpture. Directly or indirectly, the new poems discuss the vision of Hopper, Picasso, Van Gogh, Rodin, and Michelangelo. Likewise the entire volume displays Haines' wide interest and erudition. Free of the confining stereotype of Alaskan writer, the author can follow his curiosity and incorporate threads of Dante and Balzac, Catholic liturgy and Jungian psychology into the fabric of his poems.

Today it will not suffice to say that *New Poems* represents the most ambitious book of Haines' career. American poetry rarely seems short of ambition. Haines' distinction in his new book is that he matches ambition with accomplishment. He has gained in scope without losing force. He has mastered larger forms without forgetting the necessary attention to small detail. This new volume gives the reader the rare satisfaction of watching an older writer not only extend his style but perfect it.

Likewise, if I ultimately commend *New Poems* as a book of unusual artistic maturity, some readers may feel I am damning it with faint praise. Americans are not used to celebrating their poets for maturity. For every Bishop or Ransom in our literature there are a dozen *enfants terribles* (many of whom continue to be both *enfant* and *terrible* into old age). Our culture too often prizes the novel and precocious artist more than the wise and steady one. Always an uncommon man, Haines is unusual even in his virtues. He has been a slow and serious writer in a culture which celebrates speed and accessibility. Patient and tenacious, he has been more interested in perfecting his work than in popularizing it. *New Poems* is an uncompromising, often difficult book. But unlike much recent "difficult" art, it is honestly conceived and meticulously executed. If it demands study, it can also bear the weight of scrupulous attention.

But to understand these profound new poems one must turn not only to critical analysis but also to life. Like all genuine poems, they reward close reading, but they—more than most contemporary verse—also repay meditation. Haines' poetry speaks best to someone who appreciates the deep solitude out of which art arises. The attention they require is not so much intellectual as spiritual. To approach this kind of poetry one must trust it, a difficult gesture in an era like ours where so much art is characterized by pretense and vapidity. But Haines' work deserves the reader's trust. These unusual poems make the reader work, but they repay labor with spiritual refreshment. This book is not for everyone, but readers who know poetry can sometimes resemble prayer, will treasure it.

LITTLE COSMIC DUST POEM

Out of the debris of dying stars,
this rain of particles
that waters the waste with brightness...

The sea-wave of atoms hurrying home,
collapse of the giant,
unstable guest who cannot stay...

The sun's heart reddens and expands,
his mighty aspiration is lasting,
as the shell of his substance
one day will be white with frost.

In the radiant field of Orion
great hordes of stars are forming,
just as we see every night,
fiery and faithful to the end.

Out of the cold and fleeing dust
that is never and always,
the silence and waste to come...

This arm, this hand,
my voice, your face, this love.

1983

I *After* is the wrong word. It is an entirely different dimension. Time and space are crystalizations out of God. At the last hour all will be revealed.

–Martin Buber

"MEDITATION ON A SKULL CARVED IN CRYSTAL"

MEDITATION ON A SKULL CARVED IN CRYSTAL

I

To think that the world
lies wholly in this mind;
that this frozen water,
this clarity of quartz,
this ice, is all.

At home in the glass house
of wit, keeping watch
on the last conceit:

to say to oneself
in this fallen mirror
that the fog-drift of trees,
the inch of sky
in the well of windows–

These water-broken figures
entering and leaving
the last, drained pool
of light, are all.

II

Within the artifact,
in the polished brilliance
of its mirror faces,
lies the bleached horror
of the empty skull
and its loosened hinges:

of the threadlike sutures parting,
and the drained blood
dried to this rusty scale.

Think of a house abandoned
to the cold chalks that score
the limits of dust:

the ear-ports catching wind,
the long porch of the nostrils
from which the watch-beetles
and the blue, predatory flies
have long since gnawed the solitude
and eaten the silence.

And where intelligence
kept its station,
arranging interior spaces,
opening windows toward
the shellshot lunar fields,
inhuman distances...

There is nothing to see
but a small, green hollow
holding rain.

III

Where there is nothing...

But the drained stillness
of thought, the quelled
and muttering life of stones–

than which in nature
brings on inertia,
passivity, and sleep.

Wind is not welcome,
fluttering the soul of things,
nor love that makes
the shadows couple and sway.

Nothing but death is here,

windless and calm–sheer
absolution in the slow
cementing of sand grains,

glass particles that spell out,
drop by drop, the fate
of water sealed in a jar.

IV

No one the color of darkness
sees entirely the shape of the sun.

But as the ocelot goes, smoldering,
spotted with fire, through the night–

Go now, return to water and mist.
You of the fireborn, go back to rain,

be what in the beginning you were:
seed of ice and brother to grain.

You with the glass mouth, drink
more silence. Be watchful, an eye

upturned in the soil of heaven.
And every shower rebuilds your face,

at the heart of your stillness
the cry of a god trapped inside a star.

V

Blood into ice, and fur
into matted frost–
this is the way of winter,
on earth as in heaven.

Divided nostrils that smelt
of blood from afar;
the throat that drank it,
the lips and the tongue
that thirsted:

changed into that which
is shone upon, that
which mirrors, and that
which sees if looked upon.

Nothing of beast or man
remains, of the stroked fur
and the aroused flesh;
but the filed teeth fixed
in their glitter,
a smile of ferocious peace.

VI

Burn sacrifice, for all
that was clear has darkened
in the burning glass.

Break open the breast-cage,
let the creature-heart redden
in the light that remains.

Swear by the fallen blood
and burnt savor of the flesh
that the sun will rise,
that the wheel of the calendar,
carved with its lunar faces,
will never stop turning.

Put death aside,
there is nothing to fear
from the sleep-walk of spirits
in this darkness
not wholly of the night.

The great stone hall is quiet;
these pillars and dreaming cases
like a household
calmed at nightfall.

Now, as the smoke of sacrifice
disperses through chilled
and vacant rooms,
the white ash deadens and falls.

Sleep, for the changed heartbeat
knocks and is still...

In place of the lamp
that was lighted,
a drop of blood inside the sun.

VII

As if the pain of thought,
by repeated blows, would be
nothing but light in the end.

Stare into this well of shadows,
drained and never empty:
all nomenclatures, measurements
by meter and inch forgotten.

Beyond the dark slates of water
and sunlight, how the stone
jaw slides on its hinges,
how the nostrils quicken,
and the glassy brow crowns
the eyes, sunken and gleaming.

All suns, all moons, all days,
find their completion here,
as blood finds its pool of quiet
where mercury sleeps, and night
with its pallor of threads
draws the sutures closer.

The cold hours pass;
a fire-seed fumes, blown
once more into life.
The star-crossed lattice
brightens; day begins,
as empty, as filled
with floating shadows,
voices waking as before.

VIII

Of the dissolution
of fabrics and structures,
the breaking
of cemented boundaries:

Improvisations–names
that vanish among
the catalogues that vanish,
all their complexities
strung with spittle:

Hierarchies, lists of the
flowering and cheeping world:
of these and what
we knew this life to be,

death is the last confusion.

After the smoky anguish
of your dying
comes this resolution:

the opening calm, a blue
thoughtbound space
in which there are signal
lights, globed fires
giving way to night.

IX

Intelligence is what we find,
gazing into rock as into water
at the same depth shining.

Mirror, glazed forehead of snow.
Holes for its eyes, to see
what the dead see dying:

a grain of ice in the stellar
blackness, lighted
by a sun, distant within.

1977 - 86

II

Earth. Nothing more.
Earth. Nothing less.
And let that be enough for you.

–Pedro Salinas

TENDERFOOT

It is dusk back there, the road
is empty and the log house quiet.

Jessie, the Indian girl, stands
at the doorway in silence,
her thin face turned to the earth.

No more than an aching shadow,
her father bends at the sawhorse,
cutting the last dry pole.

The swallow box has fallen,
the catalogue has lost its pages.

The black mouths of the rain barrels
are telling of migrations,
the whispering rush
of a lonely people toward the past.

1962 - 82

RAIN COUNTRY

I

The woods are sodden,
and the last leaves
tarnish and fall.

Thirty-one years ago
this rainy autumn
we walked home from the lake,
Campbell and Peg and I,
over the shrouded dome,
the Delta wind in our faces,
home through the drenched
and yellowing woodland.

Bone-chilled but with singing
hearts we struck our fire
from the stripped bark
and dry, shaved aspen;
and while the stove-iron
murmured and cracked
and our wet wool steamed
we crossed again
the fire-kill of timber
in the saddle of Deadwood–

down the windfall slope,
by alder thicket, and now
by voice alone, to drink
from the lake at evening.

A mile and seven days
beyond the grayling pool
at Deep Creek, the promised
hunt told of a steepness
in the coming dusk.

II

Light in the aspen wood
on Campbell's hill,
a fog trail clearing below,
as evenly the fall distance
stretched the summer sun.

Our faces strayed together
in the cold north window—
night, and the late cup
steaming before us...
Campbell, his passion
tamed by the tumbling years,
an old voice retelling.

As if a wind had stopped us
listening on the trail,
we turned to a sound
the earth made that morning—
a heavy rumble in the grey
hills toward Fairbanks;
our mountain shivered
underfoot, and all
the birds were still.

III

Shadows blur in the rain,
they are whispering straw
and talking leaves.

I see what does not exist,
hear voices that cannot speak
through the packed
earth that fills them.

Loma, in the third year
of the war, firing at night
from his pillow
for someone to waken.

Campbell, drawing a noose,
in the dust at his feet:
"Creation was seven days,
no more, no less..."
Noah and the flooded earth
were clouded in his mind.

And Knute, who turned
from his radio one August
afternoon, impassioned
and astonished:
                    "Is that
the government? I ask you—
is *that* the government?"

Bitter Melvin, who nailed
his warning above the doorway:

Pleese dont shoot
the beevers
They are my friends.

IV

And all the stammering folly
aimed toward us
from the rigged pavilions–
malign dictations, insane
pride of the fox-eyed men
who align the earth
to a tax-bitten dream
of metal and smoke–

all drank of the silence
to which we turned:
one more yoke at the spring,
another birch rick balanced,
chilled odor and touch
of the killed meat quartered
and racked in the shade.

It was thirty-one years ago
this rainy autumn.

Of the fire we built to warm us,
and the singing heart
driven to darkness
on the time-bitten earth–

only a forest rumor
whispers through broken straw
and trodden leaves
how late in a far summer
three friends came home,
walking the soaked ground
of an ancient love.

V

Much rain has fallen. Fog
drifts in the spruce boughs,
heavy with alder smoke,
denser than I remember.

Campbell is gone, in old age
struck down one early winter;
and Peg in her slim youth
long since become a stranger.
The high, round hill of Buckeye
stands whitened and cold.

I am not old, not yet, though
like a wind-turned birch
spared by the axe,
I claim this clearing
in the one country I know.

Remembering, fitting names
to a rain-soaked map:
Gold Run, Minton, Tenderfoot,
McCoy. Here Melvin killed
his grizzly, there Wilkins
built his forge. All
that we knew, and everything
but for me forgotten.

VI

I write this down
in the brown ink of leaves,
of the changed pastoral
deepening to mist on my page.

I see in the shadow-pool
beneath my hand a mile
and thirty years beyond
this rain-driven autumn.

All that we loved: a fire
long dampened, the quenched
whispering down of faded
straw and yellowing leaves.

The names, and the voices
within them, speak now
for the slow rust of things
that are muttered in sleep.

There is ice on the water
I look through, the steep
rain turning to snow.

1979 - 83

25

III

Remember that *time* is money.

–Benjamin Franklin

DEATH AND THE MISER

I

God surely sees us,
for He sends His messengers
when we lie dying,
tugging in a repentent fever
the gold seams of a shroud.

Remember, if you can,
in your drenched delirium,
the pinched rancor of the hours
spent sorting and weighing:
the squint, the measuring grasp
fastened on dust, flake and coin.

And now the last lock is sprung,
and the domed lid
of your counting-chest stands open.

And see: the swollen purses,
rubbed and darkened leather
spilling great seals and rings;
the lure of swindled clasps
loose in their amber or ruby light.

And tossed among these,
like so many bitten leaves
tied with black thread,
the sordid bundles of credits,
foreclosures, and mean accounts
cannot be hidden.

Be sure the deadly creatures
that litter the floor
with their glittering excrement
will find you. With six and eight
polished, segmented arms
they climb the sills, horned
against the casement light.

There will never be time
to try all the keys,
nor will you be strong again
to wrestle the weight
of these belted doors that close.

So pull the shroud to your chin,
let go of your wallet
and stop your ears,
as with his steely, measuring
click
      click
            the gold-eating
beetle of death
            climbs nearer.

II

The dream within the acorn,
still green at the heart
of the forest, had more substance
than that closet-sleep of yours,
shut in by more than
natural earth and lumber.

Your rents and your reckonings,
meticulous in subtraction;
your ledger locked at nightfall,
as if all life's guilty
confusion were cancelled
by that sleeve-worn shelving
and quiet turn of a key.

From soil of soot and paper,
the sand you sifted over
the blotting ink of your days,
came neither fruit nor flower,
nothing feathered but a pen,
nor wind-shaken whisper
above the arid rustling
of your thumbed, exacting pages.

There, by candle or fretted sun,
you might have seen, as now,
flickering and doubled by fever,
your shadow-self at work,
cowled and booted,
and with great butcher's shears
slitting the rose of mercy
into a thousand tatters.

III

You would never willingly wear
the clothing of the dead,
nor touch their flesh, soured
and damp and printed with leaves.

And yet each day you have filed
and sorted the claims of death,
cut paper death in the morning,
signed ink death in the evening.

The list of death:

Ledger-death and curtain-death.
The death that studies,
that sits in chairs and stands
at counters:
                    Death the receiver.

Death in a rented cassock: cleric
and lender, the ape of stations.
And early each morning he offers
to the cold knees of penury
his wafer-death and credit-death.

For death is a shadow-priest
leaning at his slotted window;
no more than a voice, sabbath–
darkened, whispering of penance
and absolution:
> Death the confessor.

And death is waiting overhead;
he coughs, spits in the sand-wake
of voices receding. The last
of the spilled earth falls, and soon
the gardener's tread, crisp
and single on the unraked leaves.

IV

Believe in the angel beside you,
his patient and willing gesture:

> (Death with a letter
> to be delivered)

Believe in the cross, whose wood
is tinder, whose nails are rust:

> (Death with a fiery pencil
> will pierce you)

Believe in the light blown forward
from the darkness behind you:

> (Death with a windy lantern
> will find you)

Believe in the rote of numbers
chirped from the cloister at evening:

> (Death with the reed of the
> vesper sparrow is calling)

Remember: God surely sees us...
He rocks and smokes in His office:

> (Death in a quiet slipper
> will open the door)

34

V

So much leaden weight,
so much desire turned inward.

To follow without hope
of turning, the animal-reek
of one's own track...

And no one to call you back
from its steep momentum—
into the black rain
of ink, the fury of hurled
buttons and fiery quills.

And of the self-mounted
lashed to a standstill,
you too will know their anguish,
their late remorse,
who from the rank spring
of their hearts drink thirst,
only to drink again.

As yoked and branded cattle,
stunned with the blood
of the killing-floor,
they know the yelp and cutting
rein of the deputies
who ride there—masters
of pain, tyrants of the split
hoof and cloven brow.

VI

Be comforted, for your companions
go with you
down the difficult stairs.

Not creatures of your mind alone,
neither men nor women
nor angels–but stooped
and pilfering
they swarm about you
with cold beaks and probing
snouts–quarreling
rodents, insects
as large as yourself.

And their voices that are no voices,
but like the sounds of things
broken underfoot–crushed leaves
and littered shells–
thicken the air you breathe
with muddy whispers,
suppressed whines
and stifled barking.

And God is nowhere now,
if ever He watched
and crossed you
with His wand of ashes.

But waiting in their grounded flight
stand towering birds
whose outspread wings
appear to be fanning a fire,
and yet it is cold,
the frost of a thousand
winters of iron.

And deeper still as you go,
on every side
now rise before you
and fall away,
the round and rolling
shapes of gigantic coins,
tall keys with eyes
giving off sparks in the gloom...

These, and the ringing,
metallic shadows of Death,
who is himself a miser—
once he has taken,
he never gives anything back.

1980 - 84

IV

Of such may be the simplifications
that I have attempted.

–Edward Hopper

DAYS OF EDWARD HOPPER

I

These are the houses that stand,
broken and entered; these
are the walls written by rain,
the sparrow arches, the linear
stain of all that will one day
turn to smoke in the mind.

Brick dust was their pigment,
mortar and the grit of brownstone
ground underfoot, plaster
flaked to the purity of snow.

And out of these we entered
the glass arrangements of wind,
became the history of sunlit,
transient rooms, domestic shades;
a substance volatile, so thin
the light of stations burning
at the roadside consumed us...

And out of that the stillness.

II

Tell me, you who were close
to my heart, how of so
much sleep and forgetting
came that brief and
quarreling peace we knew?

From the drone and the rote
of a meticulous boredom,
only a stifled outcry
heard by the night custodian.

History was a name to give
confusion its contours—
so great a darkness of mind
scrawled with the writ
of governors, agents, and clerks,
to which we spoke aloud—
one hand on a baffled heart—
to name, but not to question.

So much for this child
of amazed colonials,
deceived as to the shore
they claimed; so much
for the citizen who
with such passion swore
allegiance to tar sands.

I think the long, barbed
shadow of a street lamp
troubled the night walker
home to his household.

I think the barber pole,
a flag without stars,
with no consoling blue,
striped the patriot
shorn in his revolving chair.

III

Obedience to Sundays drilled us
to march in the flag days
that followed; but nonetheless
were fragrant and rosy with knees,
and one could savor at recess
the evening tilt of small breasts
cupped under knitted sweaters.

The blue lines checked with red
crossed upon a page relentless
in the direction of protractors,
triangle squares: *the law of,*
the root of, the stem of...

Obedience to numbers moved us
to cherish whatever could be added
or taken away: uncertain hope
in the solace of lunch pails
and the fortune of sand lots.

All that in time was sanctified,
pure beyond all censure,
upheld our life, our sweetness
and our hope. From that strict
sodality of white wings
and black cowls, this benediction
under the rule of a handbell
rung in the red brick frost.

IV

Sleepwalker, your footsteps
long since were ground to echoes
in the glassy pavement.

Smoke was the emblem for manhood,
then as now; and *Gasoline*
the name of our country—
high octane that fueled
a tribal frenzy in the music
we danced to, the manic
vacancies we took for joy.

Our cinematic consolations
from which the Neverlands
were built—radio voices,
blackface prophecies,
tight hands and sweating lips.

But there were no words to speak
for the refused passion of a girl
standing at the porch rail
under the moth-ringed light.

We kept from the lessons learned
of many querulous masters
no more than was written
on the leaves we raked
to the curbing and burned
in the swift October night.

V

A trolley bell clangs
in the distance,
the control lights change,
and around the circle
with its chained
and blackened monument
the traffic wheels
and charges—
carriages and horses,
primitive cars.

And evening, corrosive
with inner light,
comes to the stone-slotted
benches where the elderly
are seated—
dry, catarrhal crickets,
rustling their papers,
minding their dogs.

The darkness reaches
toward them out of the trees
and flowering shrubs:
they do not see it,
not one of them understands
how soon, how swiftly,
the grass at their feet,
the paths by which they came,
the words on their lips
will vanish.

VI

And once for me also,
when quarreling whispers
were abroad, the damp wind
of an autumn night
blew the one sheer curtain
aside.
        Light that signaled
the end of a game begun
by the earth's wise children
came with its slow red pulse
to the room where I lay
awake, dismantling night.

Long knives of the shadows
slit the walls. A news-throat
muttered interrogations
at the rain-frontier: names
of the still-to-be-missing,
the sold, the bloodied
and trampled–small peace
and unforgiven crime.

                    1981 - 88

47

Somewhat closer to the heart...
but far from close enough.

–Paul Klee

HEAD OF SORROW, HEAD OF THOUGHT

You would think that no one
had the right to so much
distance and calm.

And yet how often do we see,
clouded and still,
the face of someone gone
out of himself
into stone or water?

The rider in the train,
escaped into the glass fields;
the watcher in the garden,
changed once to a leaf,
now to the cold light on a pond.

Face of the storm, we say,
we have faced you,
heard you howling within,
quelling the atoms
of a bruised, exacting heart...

She, who out of the tempest,
came to this calm,
gazing as if from a distance
made equally of granite and cloud.

1985

OF MICHELANGELO, HIS QUESTION

Sybil and prophet have spoken,
are fixed in their chairs:
Your strength was in your thought,
your dream your answer,
your consummate gift your pain.

Muscular night stands over Persia;
once more the whirlwind sweeps
the dark-tongued leaves
to the lap of a woman so old
she is a child who cannot remember
when her book of the marvelous
came unthreaded
and the pages were scattered.

Long ago the rainstorm of heaven
abated; the sun-dried witnesses
marked between the ark-ribs
God's majestic finger
stirring the dust of Adam.

A trumpet blew, one mighty event
was promised: the dead awakened,
to be ranked and divided–
the damned and the anointed,
equally made of earth.

But to stand four hundred years
in a courtyard, a pillar
for birdlime: your shoulders
warped, the stone in your hand
withheld for the one
antagonist yet to come...

Then, and only then, one's dream
would die into clay and rubble.
To prayer and petition
God speaks the simplest words:
sun, rain, and *frost.*

Here, at the end of the corridor,
where night and dawn,
dusk and noon, are gathered
in the one standing tree,
art and history
compose their towering image.

To this cloudlit stillness
the pilgrims come, reading
prayers from a guidebook–
to see, to question, and depart.

1984 - 87

ON A CERTAIN FIELD IN AUVERS

There is something in my heart...
                            –Van Gogh

I

On the road to Hallucination,
pass by the yellow house
that is the house of friendship,
but is also the color of madness...

Stand by the roadside, braced
in the punishing wind that blows
on that field and another...
In the red dust of evening,
ask yourself these questions:

'Who made the sun, strenuous
and burning?'
                    It was I.

'And the cypress, a green torrent
in the nightwind?'
                    It was I.

'And the clock of evening, coiled
like a spring?...Who turned
the stars in their sockets and
set them to spinning?'
                    It was I.

On the road to the Night Cafe,
where the light from a door
that is always open
spills over cobbles and tables;

where the pipesmoker calmed
his fury, a yellow chair
in which no one is sitting...

It is no one. It is I.

II

I, who never for one hour
forgot how the light seizes
both field and striding sower;
who held my hand steady
in the solar flame, and drank
for my thirst the fiery
mineral spirit of the earth.

Who remembered always, even
in the blistering south,
a cellar in the north
where a handful of stunted
people peeled their substance
day by day, and all their
dumb and patient misery
steeped in a cold green light.

On the road to the hospital
built of the great stones
of sorrow, and furnished
with chains and pillows...
In the red dust of evening
the Angelus is ringing.

And out among the haystacks,
strange at this late hour,
a light, both moving and still,
as if someone there was
turning, a ring of candles
burning in his hatbrim...

It is...no one.

III

In the Asylum of Saint-Rémy,
that is also the burnt field
of Auvers; at the graveside
of two distracted brothers.

On this one day in July
we speak the rites for all
torn and departed souls.

And we hope that with
a hundred years of practice
we have learned to speak
the appropriate words:

'In the country of the deaf
a one-eared man was king...

'In the name of the poor,
and of the holy insane,
and the great light of the sun.'

1986

PAOLO AND FRANCESCA

Only they who have found in love
and longing for the flesh
their entire being,
will understand this prolonged
anguish of flight
through a lasting midnight.

There was death, brother of desire,
who came with a sword.
And hate, crowned with a mighty
will. Passion's book
that was opened, and the story
once begun, lived out to the end.

And who, having met, kissed
through forbidden pages
the slime-stained mirror of love.
Who broke the glass
and followed the fire within—
hurled together
into the muttering starlight...

And such arousal as lovers know
who find in that staring
wakefulness, refusal of sleep,
vigil and consummation.

1985

BROKEN MIRRORS

...of what is not visible.
                           –Picasso

I

If what you saw of the majestic
crowing cock of the world
was loud and clear, a metallic
brightness beaked and strutting...

When in that glittering moment
illusion was still intact,
and sunlight on the glass
of the river was broken
by nothing but raindrops...

And there was coupling
in the dark of the garden
by gaslight, and all that
swirling, impetuous throng
was bright pretence,
glamor and savage paint...

What then was reality
in a world invaded by mirrors,
whose glass would break,
whose splinters pierced
the dry heart from within?

II

Into your blue forgetfulness,
distant with clowns,
silent in the wake of tumblers,
came these crippled hordes–

a thousand fractured faces
with stunned eyes that strayed
from corner to corner,
to be fixed in a brutal stare
that had no smile behind it...

As if all of humanity's clipped
cartoons and holy discards–
composure of sleek madonnas,
breasts and buttocks, the leaping
limbs of centaur and faun–
were hacked and crumpled,
shaken in a box, and a voice
in all that litter cried out:

III

"I...I... am the woman,
the face on the playing card,
I the lightbulb, and I
the skull of a stricken horse...

"I sit in a room with no one
to talk to, I play the clown,
ride the circus bicycle
round and around in a circle...

"I dance where the splinters
are green, I break into smaller
and smaller needles of red...
But I stop, stop in my giddy

"gyrations–Stop, listen
to the blind guitarist
who goes on playing, though
his music cannot be heard."

IV

But when all these shattered
faces are halfway mended,
and the horrible, stabbing beak
of the world is blunted,

you return once more
to an enormous blue room,
where the clowns are distant
and the wheels are still.

Dazed and famous
in your small white age,
you will sit by the hour,
to stare with filmed eyes

on the one bright image composed.

1986

THE OWL IN THE MASK OF THE DREAMER

Nothing bestial or human remains
in all the brass and tin
that we strike and break and weld.

Nothing of the hand-warmed stone
made flesh, of the poured heat
filling breast, belly, and thigh.

The craft of an old affection
that called by name the lion shape
of night, gave rain its body

and the wind its mouth–the owl
in the mask of the dreamer,
one of the animal stones asleep...

By tinker and by cutting torch
reduced to a fist of slag,
to a knot of rust on a face of chrome.

So, black dust of the grinding wheels,
bright and sinewy curl of metal
fallen beneath the lathe:

Speak for these people of drawn wire
striding toward each other
over a swept square of bronze.

For them the silence is loud
and the sunlight is strong.

No matter how far they walk,
they will never be closer.

1984

ANCESTOR OF THE HUNTING HEART

There is a distance in the heart,
and I know it well–
leaf-somberness of winter branches,
dry stubble scarred with frost,
late of the sunburnt field.

Neither field nor furrow,
nor woodlot patched with fences,
but something wilder: a distance
never cropped or plowed,
only by fire and the blade of the wind.

The distance is closer than
the broomswept hearth–
that time of year when leaves
cling to the bootsole,
are tracked indoors,
lie yellow on the kitchen floor.

Snow is a part of the distance,
cold ponds, and ice
that rings the cattle-trough.

Trees that are black at morning
are in the evening grey.
The distance lies between them,
a seed-strewn whiteness
through which the hunter comes.

Before him in the ashen snow-litter
or the village street
an old man makes his way,
bowed with sack and stick.

A child is pulling a sled.

The rest are camped indoors,
their damped fires smoking
in the early dusk.

                                        1983

VI

...The naked trees,
The icy brooks, as on we passed, appeared
To question us, "Whence came ye, to what end?"

–Wordsworth

WATER OF NIGHT

I

Before any match was struck
or a candle lighted,
someone spoke well of the sun.

There were bones to read
while the long dusk lasted,
marrow to force with a stick.

Feather of auk, beak of owl,
were tools to work the shadows,
make the winter hawk fly
and the stone ox stand.

As sparks fly seaward
from a beaten driftlog,
telling the days of a journey...

So from its mitten a hand
cracked with frost
parted the mosswick flame,
to read in a shoulderblade
the source of smoke
and meaning of the wind.

Nothing was written for the snow
to keep or the water
to carry, nothing to be forgotten.

And one man late in his years,
by light of the sun
through a wall of ice,
carved from ivory
a weasel the length of his finger.

II

The night people called to the shadows,
and the shadows awoke–
came down from the rafter clearings

in the light that came at sundown,
slowly basking,
from the fires at earth's end.

The night people spoke in whispers,
or with the cries of storm-driven birds
–wings in the darkness overhead,
bearing homeward the souls of the dead.

And the dead were awake, upright
and listening,
in the tread of the striding wind.

*

Then came the steady lamp,
and the reader
solitary in his pages.

The night people fell silent,
their lips were crushed,
shadows flew home from the walls...

Light, abundant light
has killed them, great books
have put them to sleep.

III

From a few rocks ground into powder,

refined sugars dissolved
burning on our tongues,
from a yellow, corrosive flour
we made our bread.

Our crumbs and our crusts,
thrown out, blew away...

to the feet of the sparrows
who pecked them,
to the knees of the homeless
who clutched them.

It was part of what we did not know
and put aside,
a bread better eaten in silence
with greying faces.

From these once more
came death,
by water, by wind.

Invisible dust from within
began to eat up our bodies.

IV

When the people of shadow
were burned,
their ashes changed into flies
and stinging swarms.

Full of blood as winter came,
they returned to the earth
and slept.

And so the deep changes when on:
fingers into roots,
and rocks from their clinging bones.

But the people of shadow
would not lie still;
they shouldered their atoms under snow

for the sweating farmer come back
with the sun
to break his furrows.

Each turn of his plow,
a swarm of ashes
rained upward from the ground.

V

After the burden of soil
was set aside,
and the scouring shovels halted,

in the great trenches
a little rain fell,
soaking the coal dust.

A wind came over that land
and its white hills moved,
the thin grass seeded there
could not hold on.

Slowly, like a surf on the plains,
tumbling and foaming,
pushing the farms,
the battered, unpeopled towns:

houseframe and headboard,
grey barns shattered to lumber,
with snarls of stockwire
bound into tossing bales...

Came on with blowing sand
and stones rolling,
with nothing to stop them,

into the souring trenches,
the black ravines.

VI

We who found work for the dead
knew how to build,
from the clay of the land
and the lime of their bones.

Effigies in mud stood by
and watched us, cemented in labor:
little teeth, glinting nails,
and the bones remembered.

They ate into the silence
of the priests, studied oppression
in the bowls of the beggars;
gnawed and listened
until the halls blew empty.

Famine, wind of the prophecies,
a dryness invading the fields;
great, smothering trees
climbed the eroded chancels.

Strange men who read the past
stopped here with pencils,
deciphering shells, to be told
by a grimace from the leaves
how all this dust went by:

We, the stone herdsmen,
driving before us in a fever
the cattle of rock
and the sheep of sand.

VII

Fire that was sunlight
blackened in the fields of earth,
dry lake and smoldering reef,
deep fernwood drowned in night.

A saw-tooth locked in that grain,
the shell body of a beetle
still rasps in tundra pools.

Seeds, brown flesh of leaves:
an old fragrance of the forest,
a sour reek and ash
blown down from chimneys.

VIII

Each of us brings a shadow,
another self we carry
as long as we walk in the sunlight,
and a dead thing's shadow dies.

Dry heads of thistles
make a shadow,
the stretched figure of a man
standing or striding,
wire, and a blade of straw.

Shadows into pools, and pools
into lakes flood back,
windlass ropes hauling darkness
out of foaming wells:

comes up with sound of frogs
and the night cries of birds,
strong blood of something
killed in the earth.

And these shadows are climbing,
big hands on our walls,
sticking and sucking...

Over the drowned gullies,
houses, fields of the earth,
seething and rocking,
water of night.

1977 - 82

VII

...Believe me, he alone
is interesting who still
loves something.

– Jacob Burckhardt

IN THE FOREST WITHOUT LEAVES

I

In the forest without leaves:

forest of wires and twisted steel...

The seasons are of rust
and renewal,
or there are no seasons at all,

only shadows that lengthen
and grow small–
sunlight on the edge of a blade.

Nothing that thrives, but metal
feeding on itself–

cables for roots,
thickets of knotted iron,
and hard knots of rivets
swelling in the rain.

Not the shadows of leaves,
but shadows where the leaves might be.

II

What sounds can be heard
in a forest without leaves?

The freezer-mutter that talks us
to sleep:

The teeth in the rubber-chatter
that nip us and wake us:

From zone to zone, veering
and halting, a frantic bleating
from the sheep-wagons:

The road-hounds, red-eyed
and yelping:

And over the tree-tops,
snorting fire,
gas-bark and chopper-bite:

Wired and winking in sleep,
even the deaf repeat
the bright, green chirp
of the dial-crickets:

Da-deet, da-deet,

     Da-deet, da-deet...

III

This earth written over with words,
with names, and the names
come out of the ground,
the words like spoken seeds.

What field, what dust,
what namesake for a stone
that moves by inches
and clears a path in the mud?

Ice moved once, a river of stones,
and the road it drove
through the forest can still be walked.
Look there–you will find
for your house a standing boulder.

Earth worn deep by its names,
written over with words:

there are spaces inside those words,
and silence for the clearing
where no house stands.

IV

One rock on another,
that makes a wall.

One field by another,
one house and another:
smoke, and the
dungfires at evening.

Voices, tread of a loom
in a doorway,
one thread and another.

A stick in the ground
and a hole for the seed,
and one stone
rolled on another.

One child and another,
one death by another:
earth, and the
funeral pyre at evening.

The men of mud
came to plow,
the people of dust
will harvest.

V

Earth speech:

the furrow sighing
behind the plow,
the clods talk together.

Mobs of dust protest
in whispers,
pushed on by the wind,
and the spilled sand
hisses, going by.

Talus, those rough words
spoken by mountains
growing old;
young pebble voices
make noise underfoot.

The cry of a rock
loosened in the night
from the cliffs above,

rolling past.

VI

And sometimes through the air
a cone of dust,
once flower, tree, or child...

Takes sudden fire across a field,
a running shape
that falls to nothing in the wind.

You cannot say what name it had.

And sometimes through the air
this dust is like a willow
tethered to a cloud...

It burns before us, glittering
in the sun,
to vanish on the road.

And sometimes through the air
a thing of dust...

VII

Say after me:

I believe in the decimal,
it has divided me.

From my tent of hair
and the gut-strings that held it;
from my floor of grass
and my roof of burning cloud.

I have looked back across
the waste of numerals–
each tortured geometry
of township and lot–

to the round and roadless vista,
to the wind-furrow
in the forest track,
when I had myself entire.

Say after me:

That freedom was weight and pain,
I am well-parted from it.

Earth was too large
and the sky too great.

I believe in my half-life,
in the cramped joy
of partitions,
and the space they enclose.

VIII

Building with matches,
pulling at strings,
what games we had.

Monopolies, cartels,
careers in the wind,
so many tradesmen of dust.

Steam in the kettles,
blades in the cotton–
big wheels went round.

And soon there was nothing
but lots and corners,
the world chopped to pieces.

Each piece had a name
and a number,
thrown in a box:

games given to children,
they too might learn
to play–
grow old and crooked,

fitting the pieces,
pulling at strings.

IX

Those who write sorrow on the earth,
who are they?

Whose erased beginnings still
control us–sentence
by sentence and phrase by phrase,

their cryptic notations vanish,
are written again
by the same elected hand.

Who are they?

Remote under glass, sealed
in their towers
and conference rooms–

Who are they?

Agents and clerks, masters
of sprawl–
playful men who traffic in pain.

Buried in their paragraphs,
hidden in their signatures–

Who are they?

X

Life was not a clock,
why did we always measure
and cramp our days?

Why the chain and why
the lock,
and why the chainman's tread,

marking acres and stony squares
out of the green
that was given?

To see in a forest
so much lumber to mill,
so many ricks to burn;

water into kilowatts,
soil into dust,
and flesh into butcher cuts–

as we ourselves are
numbered, so many factors
filed in a slot.

Say after me:

The key that winds the clock
turns a lock
in the prison of days.

XI

How the sun came to the forest:

How the rain spoke
and the green branch flowered:

How the moss burned
and the wasp took flight,
how the sun in a halo of smoke
put an end to summer.

How the wind blew
and the leaves fell.

Death made a space in the forest
where snow would come,

and silence, and night.

XII

In all the forest, chilled
by its spent wealth,

in the killed kingdom of grass
where birch leaves
tumble and blow;

(and over the leaves is written:
how great the harvest,
how deep the plow)

I know one truth:

Nothing stains like blood,
nothing whitens like snow.

XIII

What will be said of you,
tree of life,
when the final axe-blow
sends your great wood crashing?

Something about the wind upstairs,
that tromping and thrashing
on a roof never still?

What of the rift in your rafters
parting, your nests
and shingles flying?

What trace of your winter shadow,
but a lean, fantastic spider
sprawled and knotted in the snow?

And no one left to tell
of your heartwood
peeled down to a seed of ash,
your crowned solitude
crushed to a smoldering knot...

The ages parted to let you fall,
and a tall star blazed.

XIV

A coolness will come to their children,
the solar wind falling calm,
a stillness in the sun.

The poles swing wide into darkness,
there is ice in that distance.

In the deep stone shell of the suburbs
candles are stirring,
a tallowy stain on the drifts.

Humanity thinned to an ancient hardness
strikes scant fire
from the wood of buried houses,
speaks of soil and spring
with frost-thickened tongue.

It is equinox, the time of old calendars,
when birds set out on their polar journeys,
whales turned north,
men thought of the plow and the net.

Snow is falling, the sun is late,
and someone has gone with a lantern
to search the roads.

XV

In the forest without leaves
stands a birch tree,
slender and white.

For the sun drank pallor
from its leaves,
and the marrow in its roots
froze down.

Only the paper bark stayed
to weather and peel,
be sunlight or tinder
burned in the hunter's fire,

and wind took away all the rest.

If and whenever we come again,
I will know that tree.

A birch leaf held fast
in limestone ten million years
still quietly burns,
though claimed by the darkness.

Let earth be this windfall
swept to a handful of seeds–
one tree, one leaf,
gives us plenty of light.

1977 - 84